The Art of Sri Town

By RL Lane

"Where is Sri Town?" I asked.

"I do not know." I replied.

"Is it where the magical falls are?" I asked.

"Oh. No, it's not. Those are in Chittinango." I corrected myself.

"Well, I am intrigued by the name. I wonder what it means." I thought.

"Sri. We already told them the meaning in EcarreT." I said.

"I know, but we are missing something about the name…" I insisted.

"You can reverse the letters and get Sir." I pointed out.

"Sir Town? His town? Whose town?" I asked.

"Oh. My soul mate's" I said. "He is coming!" I exclaimed.

I had been sitting by the altar looking at the stained glass window inside my church earlier that day when I drew the first water color painting…

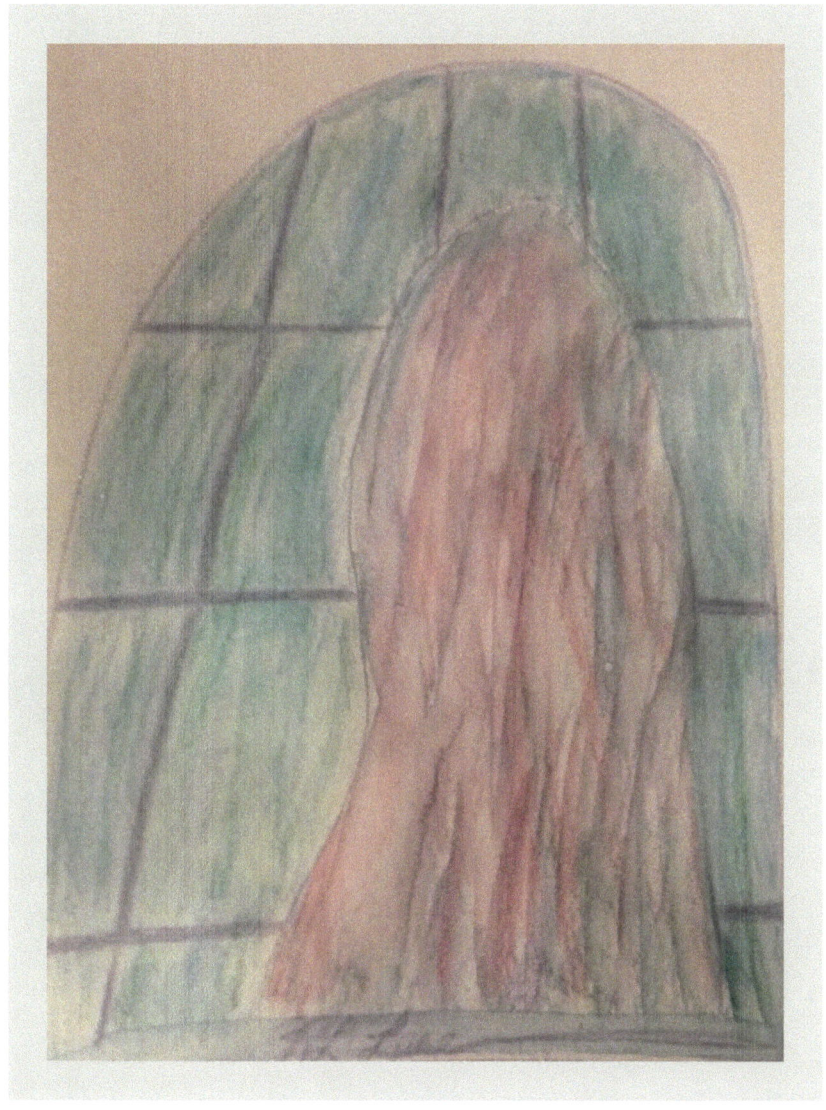

The girl looking at the window.

The girl looking out the window?

The book of light…her book of light made me really happy. I had hoped it would shed some light on all these mysteries…

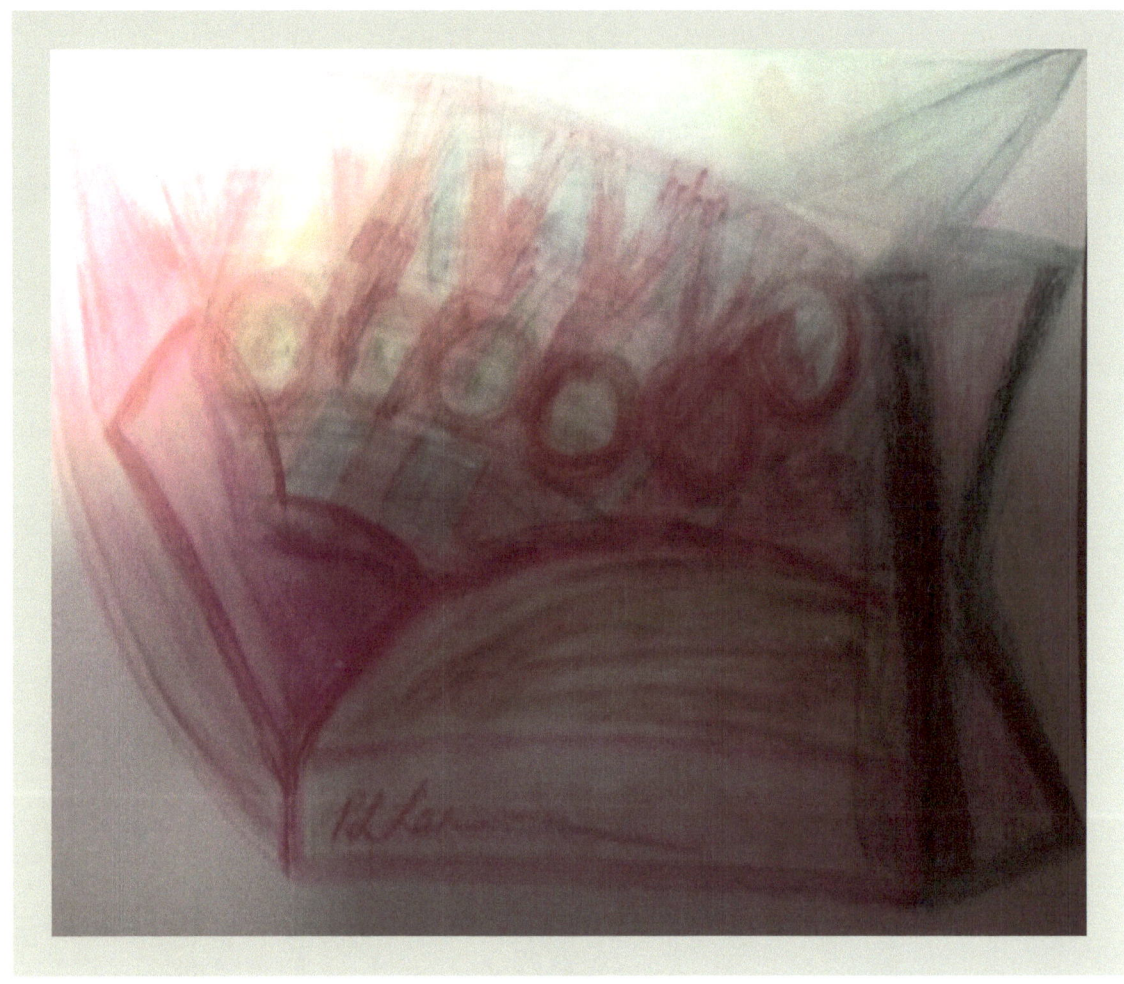

We figured out who shot JFK and how evolution works and where the missing plane is…

We drew a plane, but this one had been hit and the wing torn apart…

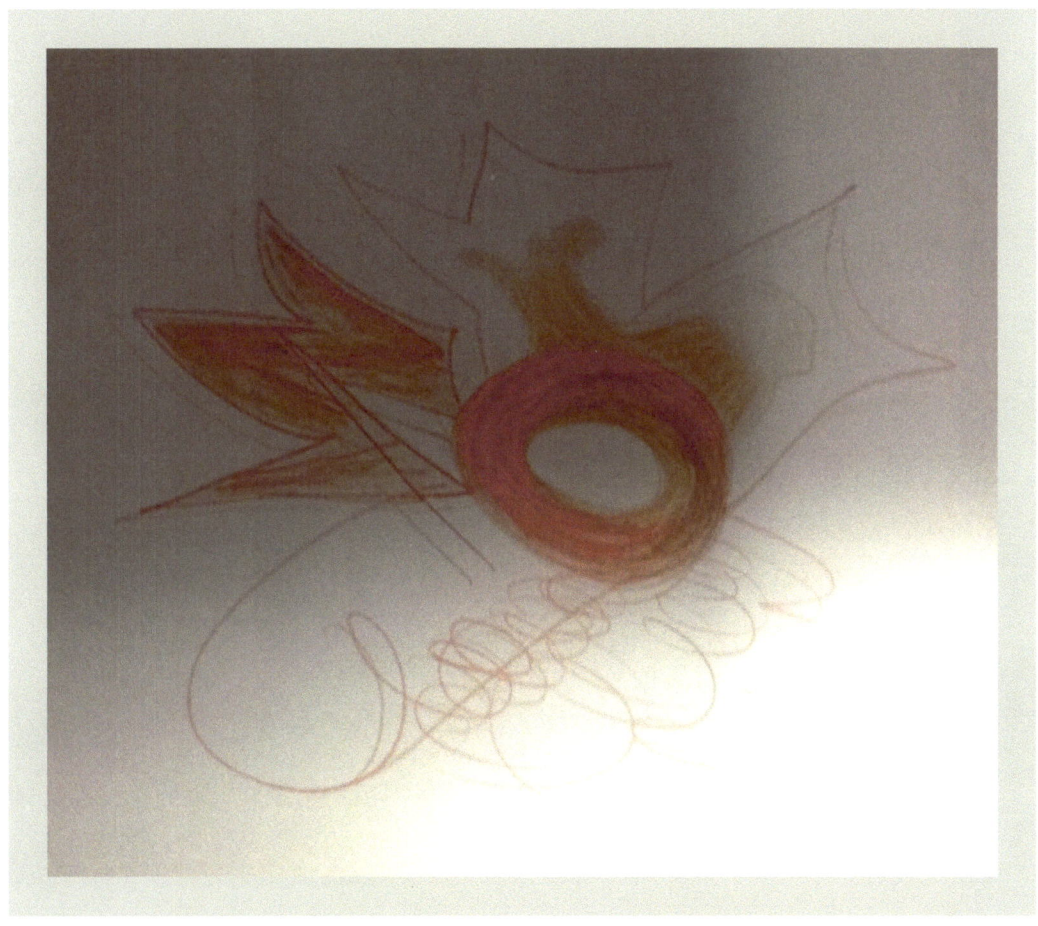

I hope to not draw any of these before my future plane trips.

I loved this one. The big ring on her hand. The church doors where she would walk down the long aisle in her sister's white dress…

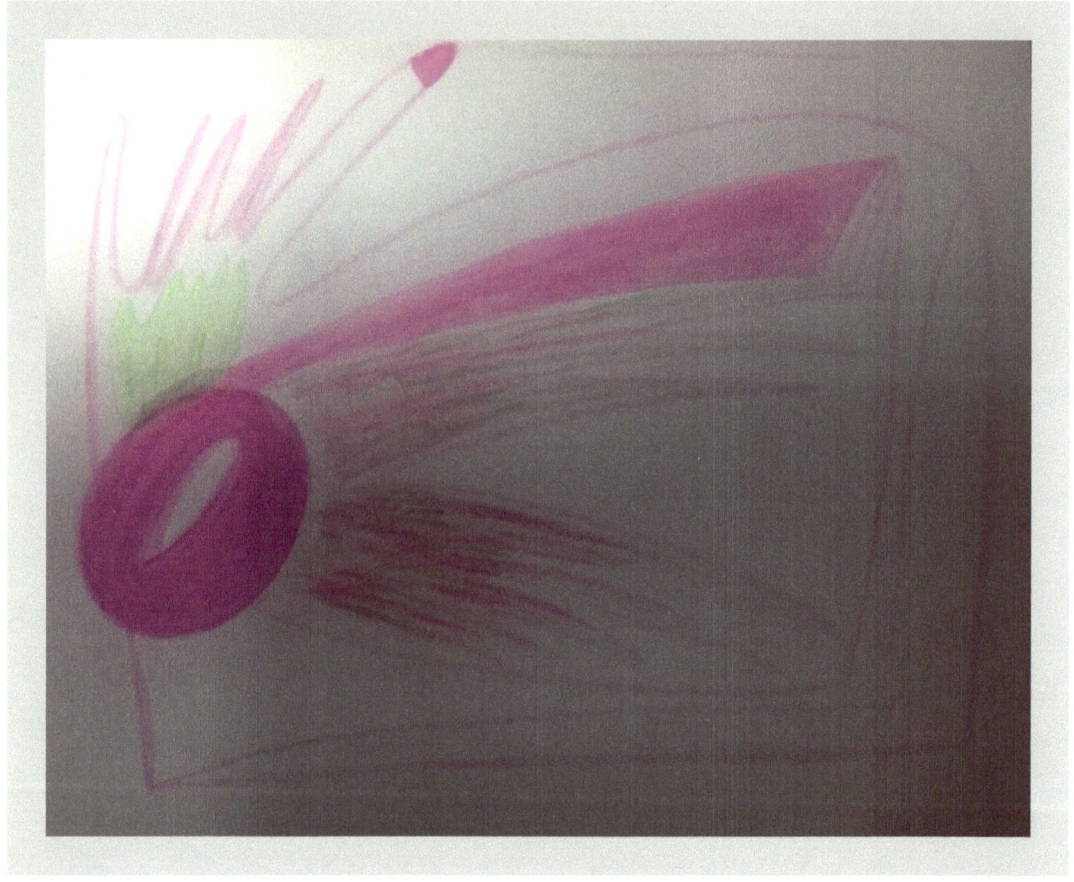

RL Lane doesn't care about the shiny things, but she will let herself have the big rock because it will remind her of the rock that she writes about in EcarreT. It will remind her of her Dad's boxing name, "The Rock". It reminds her of her last book of her life, "The Rock".

It will remind her to never give up

To fight till the end

For the things that are worth

Fighting for

Love is worth

Fighting for.

I called this the mountain façade. I see the lily, the face. The caves…

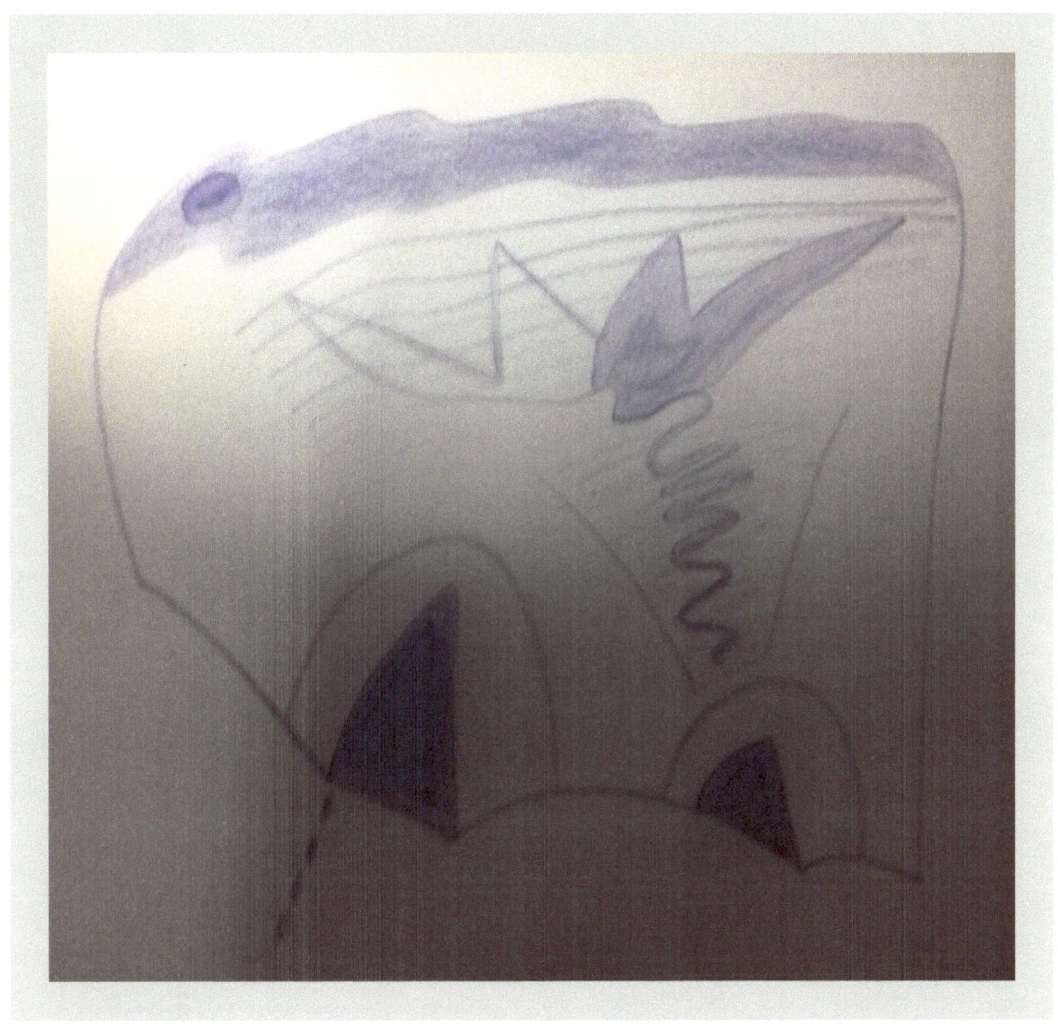

4 people are walking into the cave. Just like on the front cover. 4 people are walking into the cave entrance…

This drawing is on your back cover. It is not in "Sri Town". It is first shown in "Which of EcarreT". #4 in the EcarreT series…

"I was standing on the old wooden chair reaching up to hang the picture on the wall. It said "Memories" and had a picture of the two girls when they were young standing in front of an ice cream truck. My daughter and her cousin. I had slippers on. The chair was shaky. *Oh no. No. She had slippers on that day? The day she fell. Why? Why didn't she put on sneakers? She had sneakers. Why didn't she use a ladder? Did she have a ladder? She was in a hurry. She wanted to get something. In a hurry. In a hurry. Time is ticking by…"* Excerpt from "Which of EcarreT".

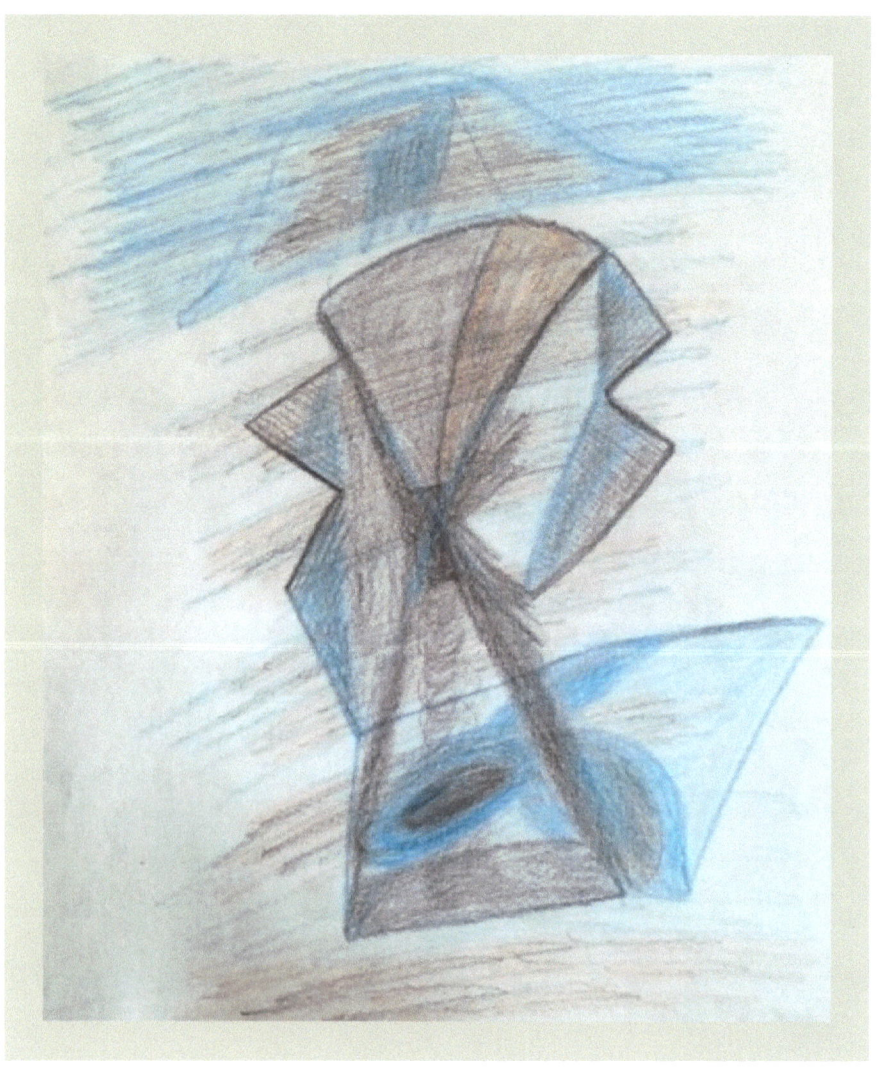

It is the book with the little green house…

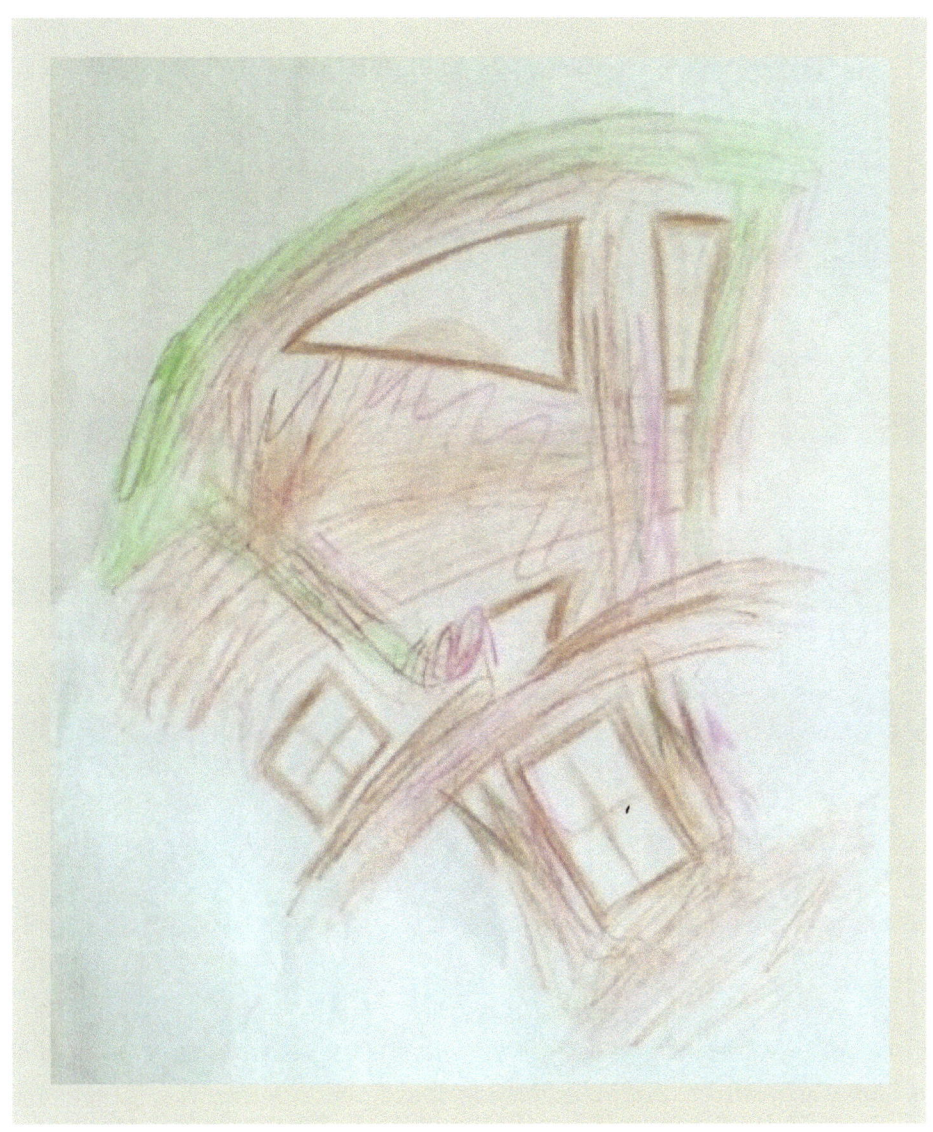

Does it come alive? Are all houses alive? Do we make them

come alive?

There is another house being sucked in by the storm…

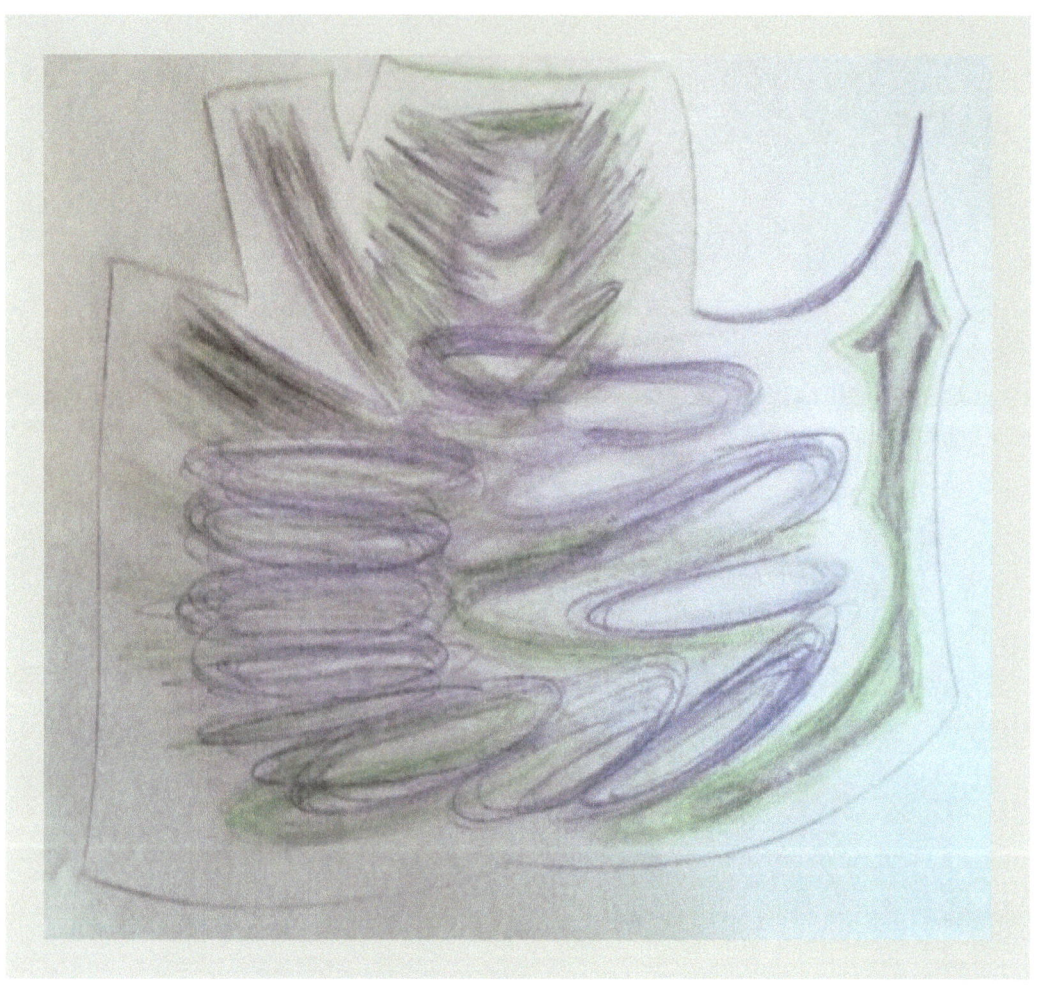

This one confused me. Mr. Storm looks happy. Oh. He would be happy. That is his job. To destroy. Take down the houses…carry them away. Is this Mr. Tornado?

Who is she? I see diamonds. Are they rabbit feet? Her hair is a long mess. She is all frazzled. Oh. She is me…

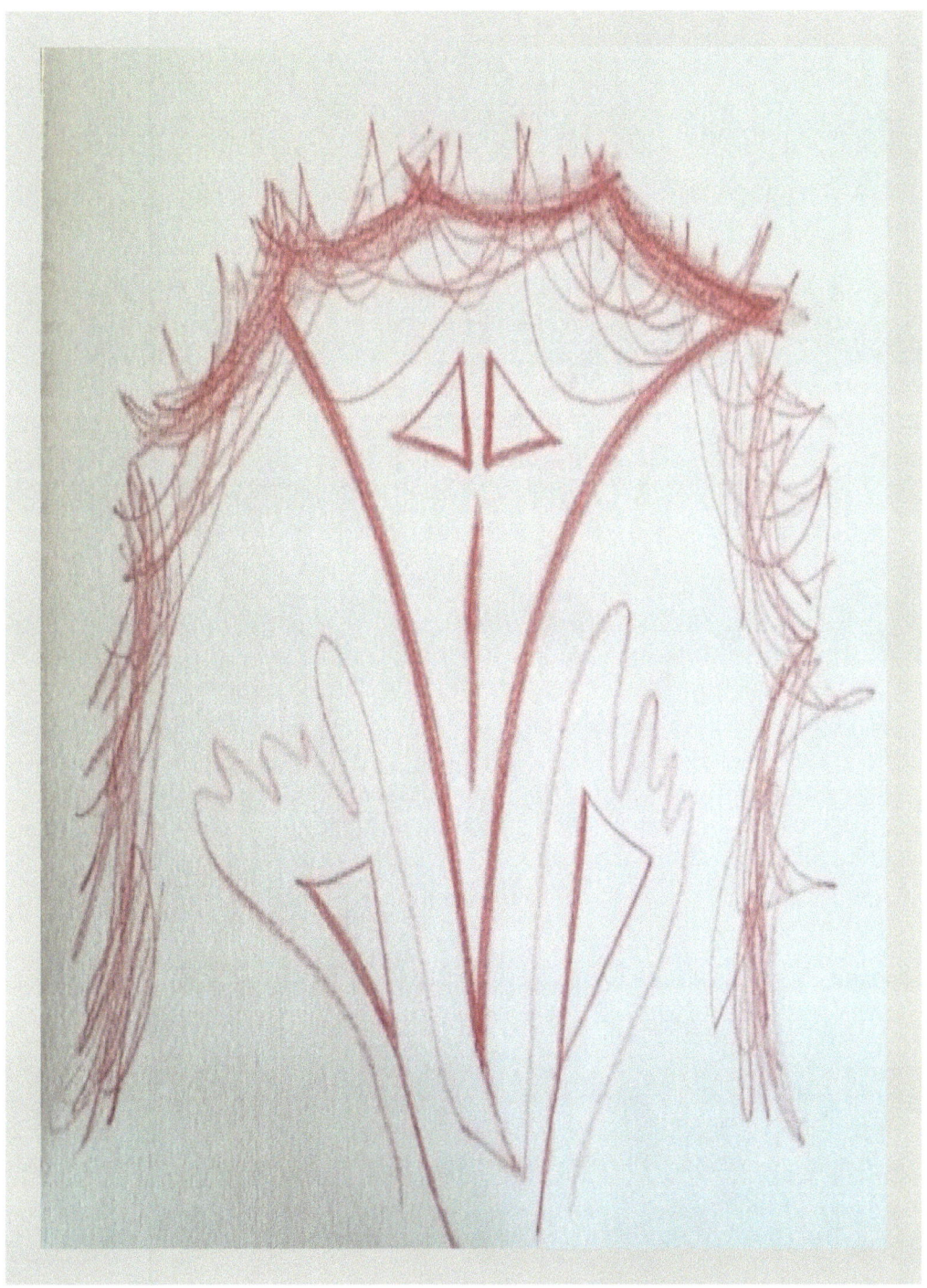

Will cupid spare an arrow to find her love? She does already have one love. Her books…

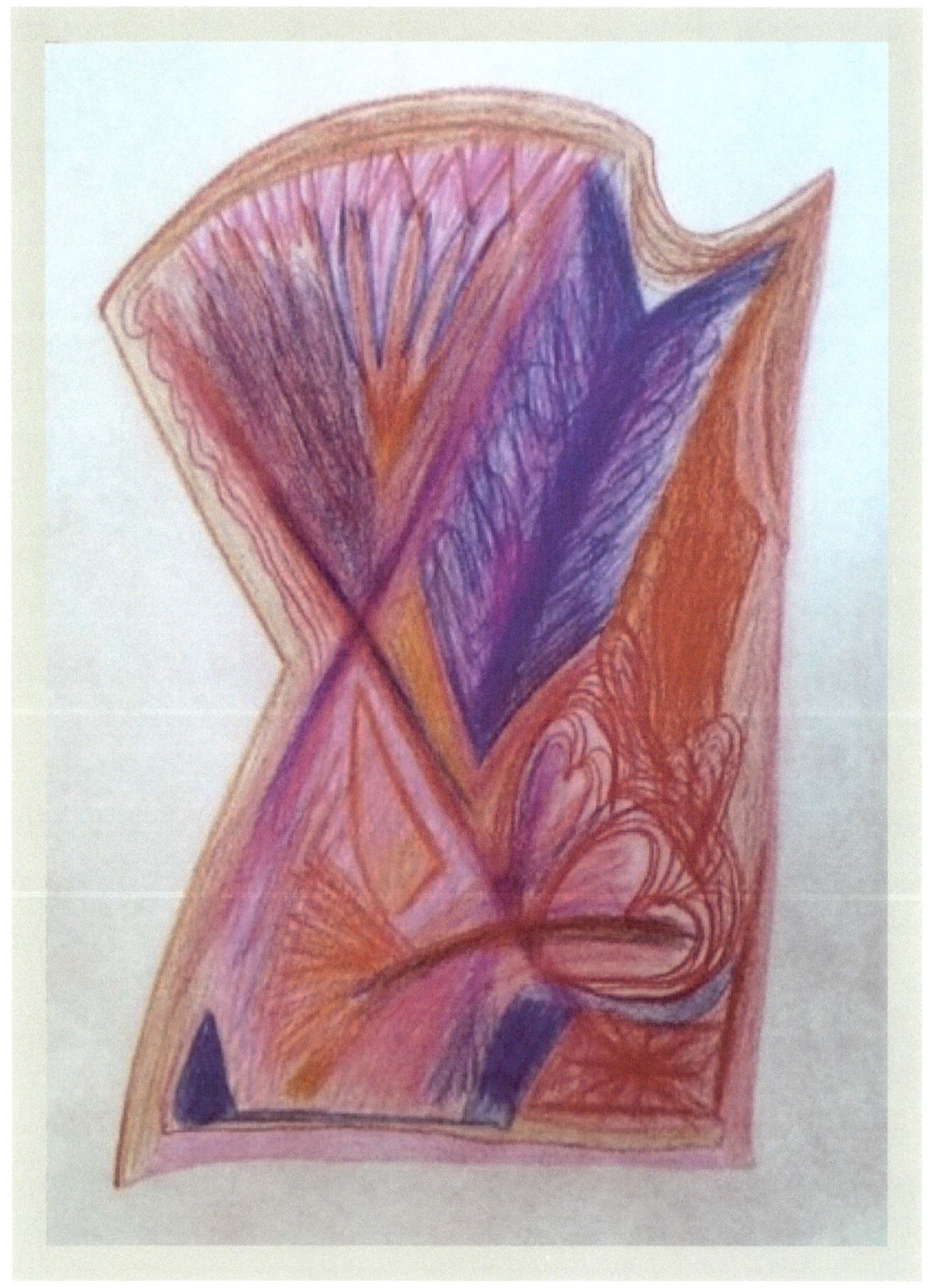

She doesn't want a part-time love. She wants a love forever. One with fireworks and with someone who will stand beside her. Is she leaning against him?

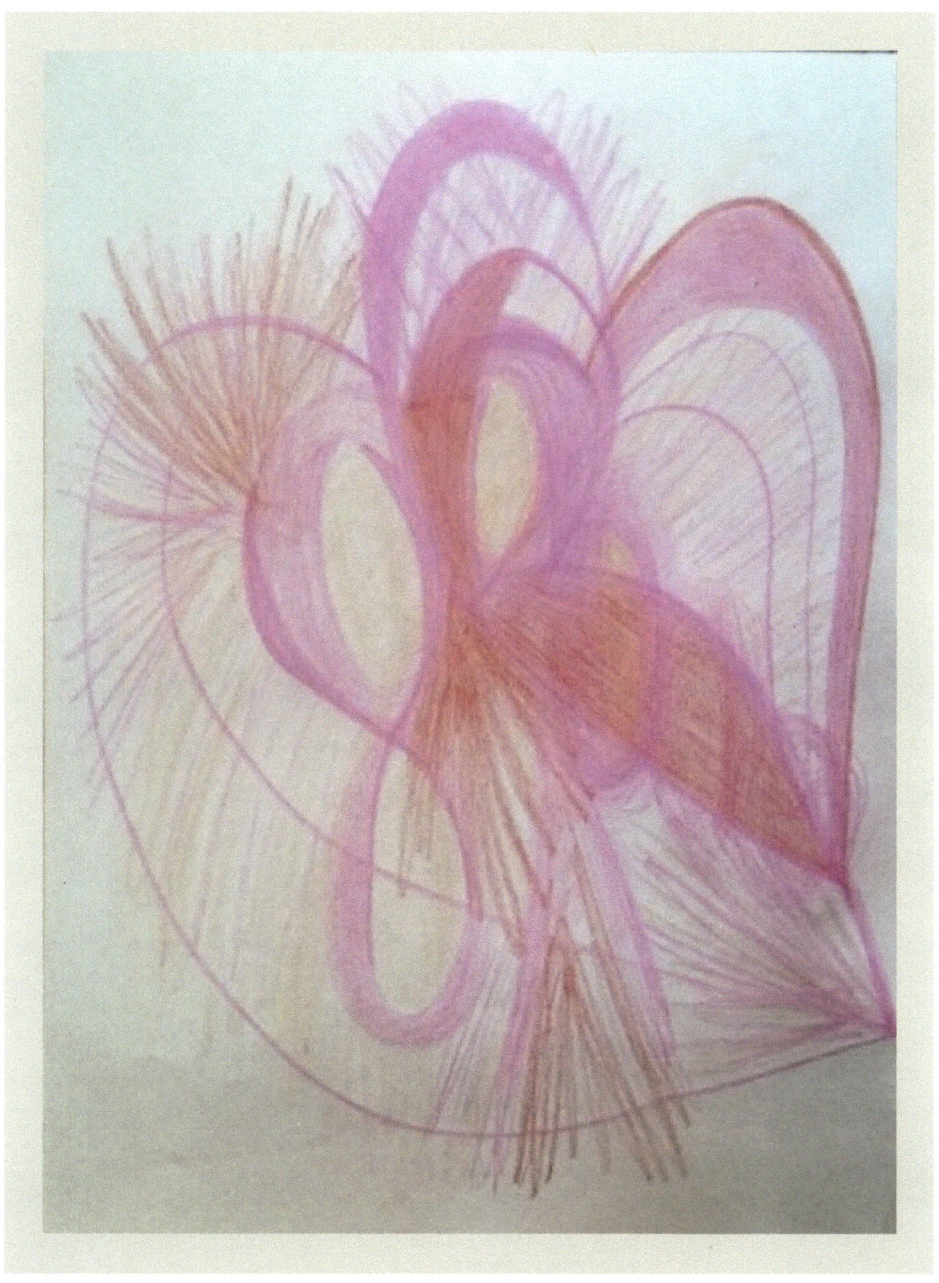

If she draws it will it become real? Is she drawing it because it is going to become real?

She still doesn't know who The Shiek is or even why she calls him The Shiek…

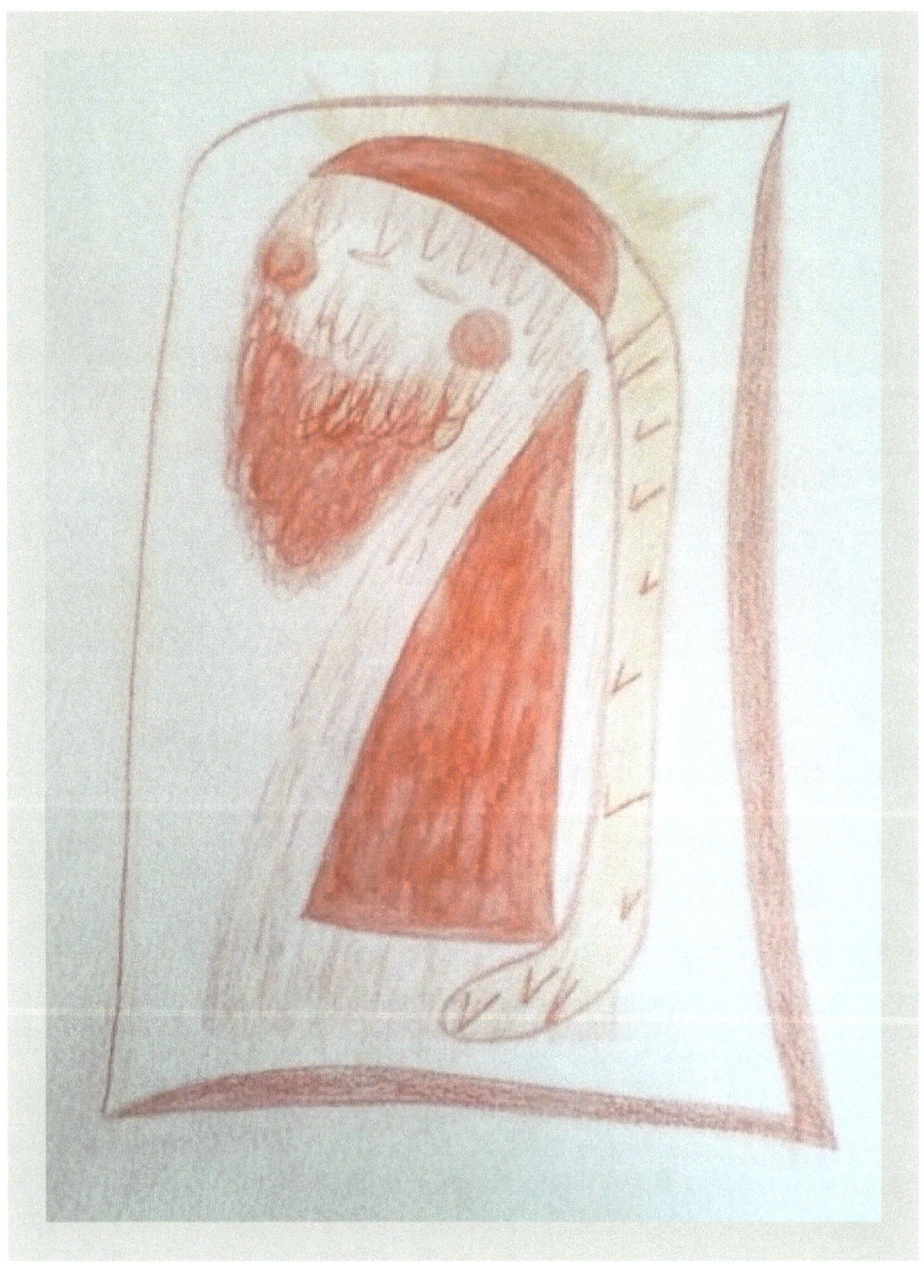

Why is he drawn on a page? Why does he have that stocking cap? Why is he glowing like an angel? He is not St. Nicholas with his rosy cheeks but who is he? It is one of her biggest questions.

Something happened in 1968. I see the red XO. Did the paths really meet again? What happened that they would never cross again?

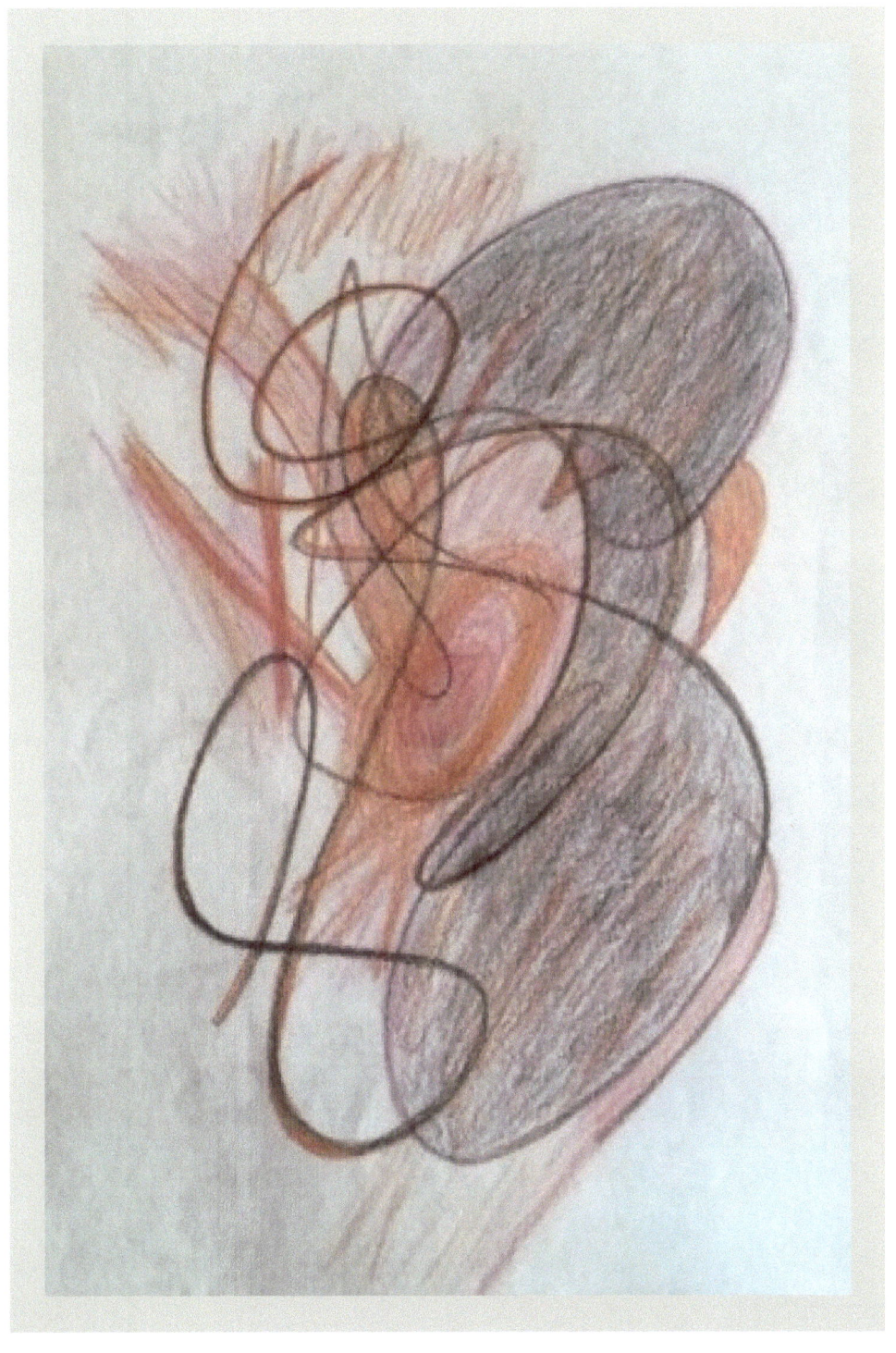

That meeting could have been the one event that grew the family tree. The one that would shortly thereafter grow the little girl. The one you first meet at the beginning of "Chapel Street Signs"…

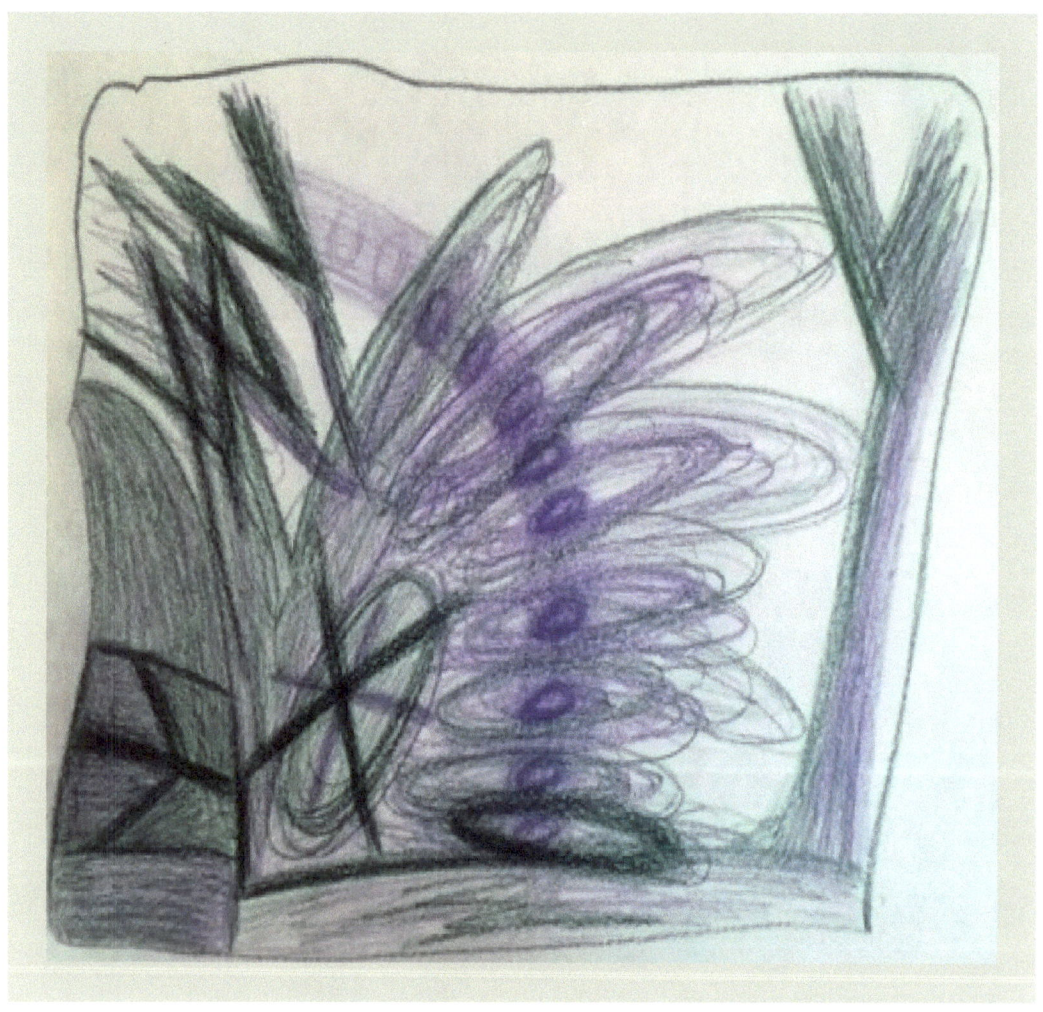

Something reminds me of an Indian headdress.

She hasn't yet figured out where the Indian connection is. Perhaps she needs her soul mate for that part of the story…

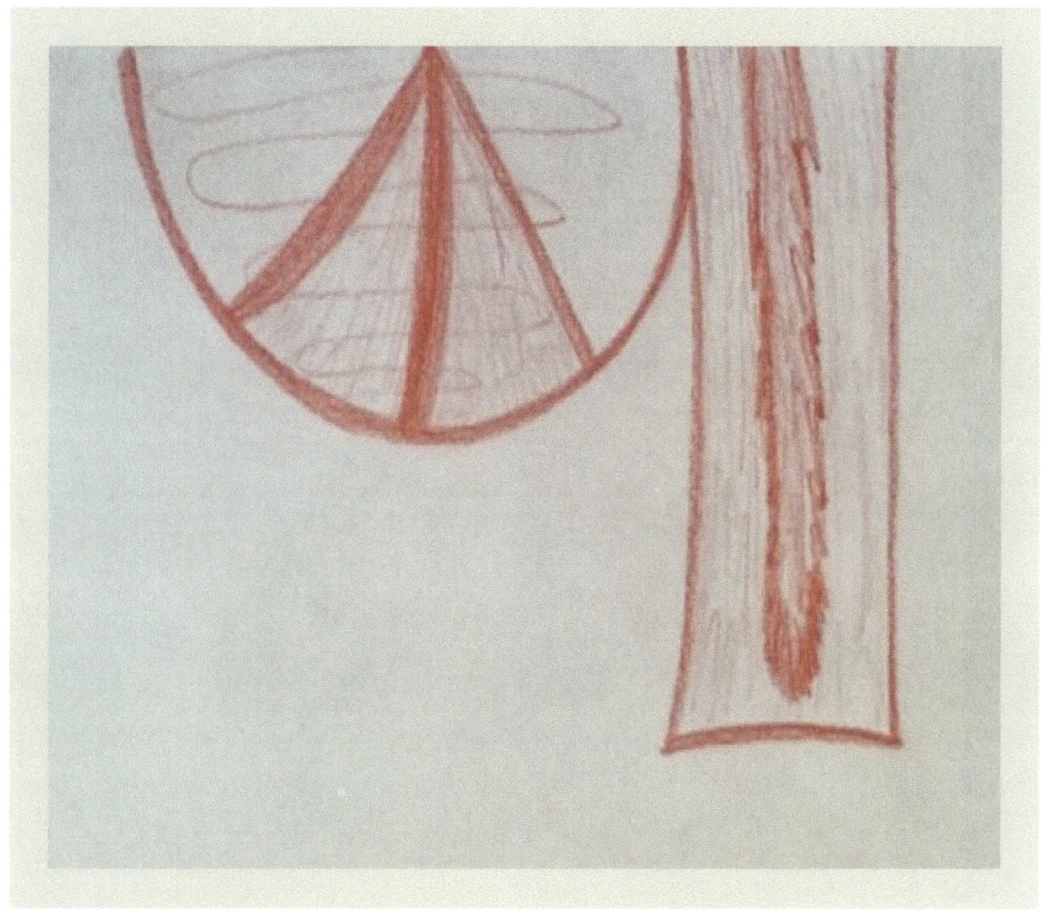

The smoke of their peace pipes, how they lived the land. The tribes that helped each member. Where…were they the last ones to know what a family was?

Where are they now?

Do they hide from us?

Ashamed to be a part of us.

Why are the birds sad now? They still sing their songs, but no one listens. They still sit in trees, but no one sees them…

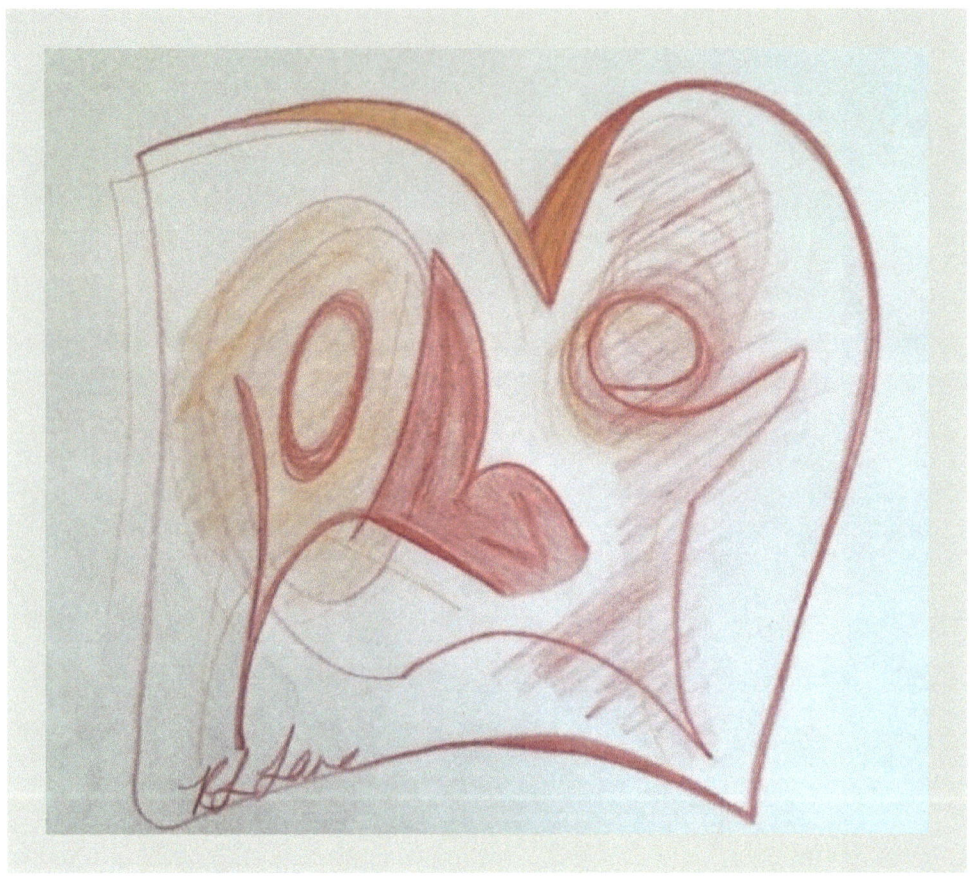

There is another animal in this picture. I am not sure what it is. I keep thinking there is a pig somewhere. I do see all the letters of love.

The sailors from the ships…or were they pirates? Do they look down confused and sad? Wondering how we lost all the honour? All the hours that pass us by with no honor.

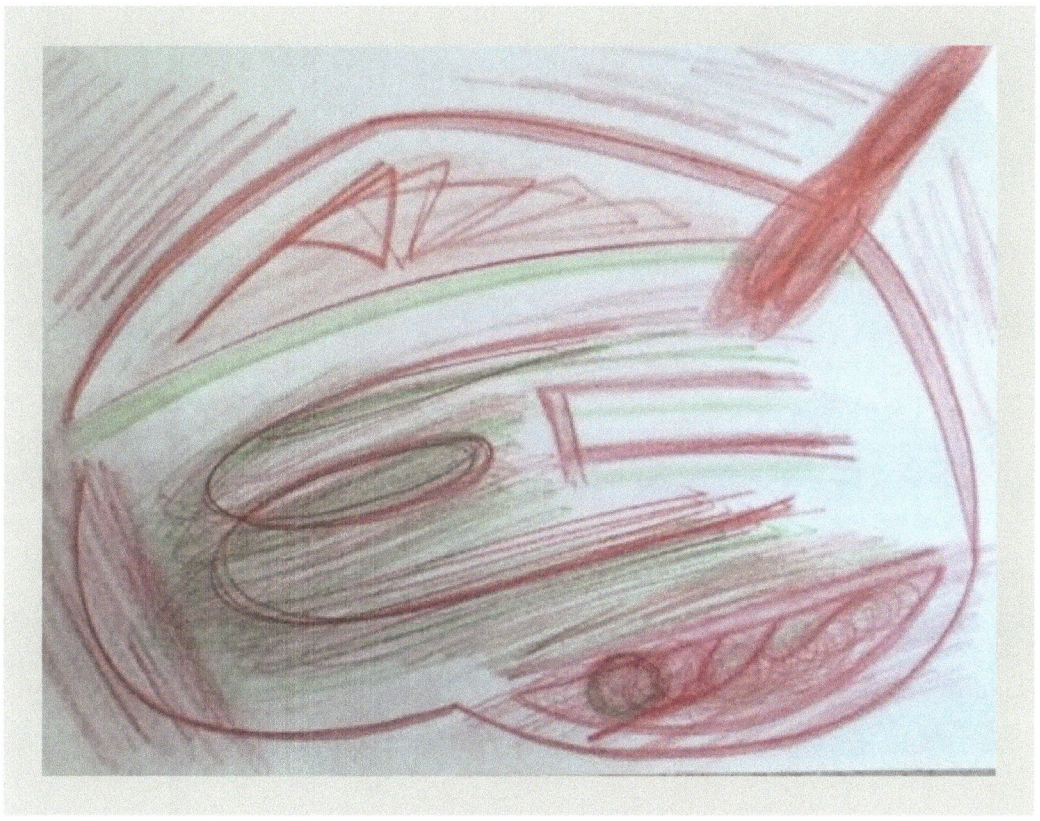

At the top, the flag has fallen down.

She we...will raise it again? That is her question. Can she help to raise it again?

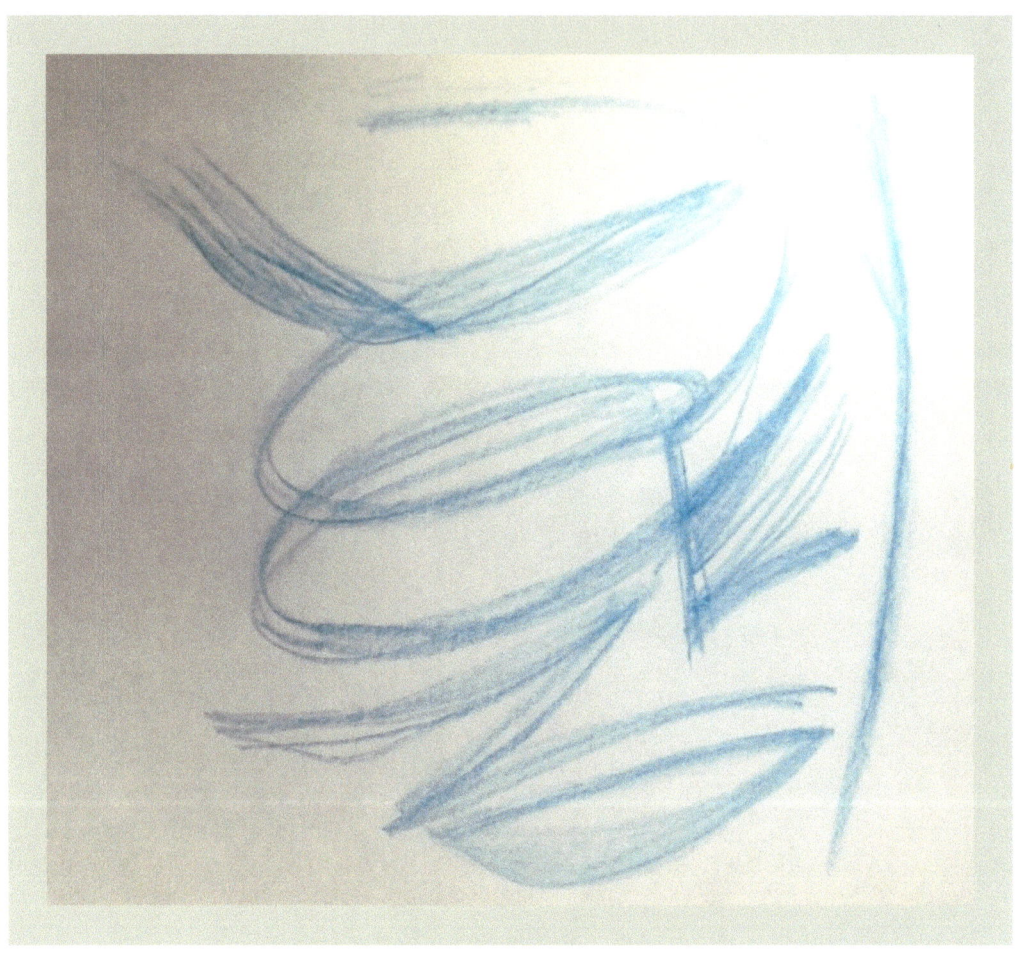

But she is nobody. Just a girl with a name.
Why did they call upon her to sort out this mess?

She was just going along

In a mundane life...

"I love the things that cannot be explained. They challenge us. They strain our minds, bend our hearts, and open our eyes. Even better yet, I love when the unexpected occurs. The unexpected in a mundane life. A life well on its course takes a turn in a direction that a month prior could have never been seen or even dreamed. "Do you believe in spirits?" I asked my friend. "Ghosts, you mean?" he replied. "No…spirits of people who have died." "Well look", he said, "I believe there are things that can't be explained." That was all I needed to hear…and I began to pour out ALL my stories…" Excerpt from "Chapel Street Signs". The beginning.

And pour I did. I will be almost up to 300,000 words by the end of "Hand of Heven".

I tried to stomp…stop. I couldn't. Rosalie Lane. RL Lane was born.

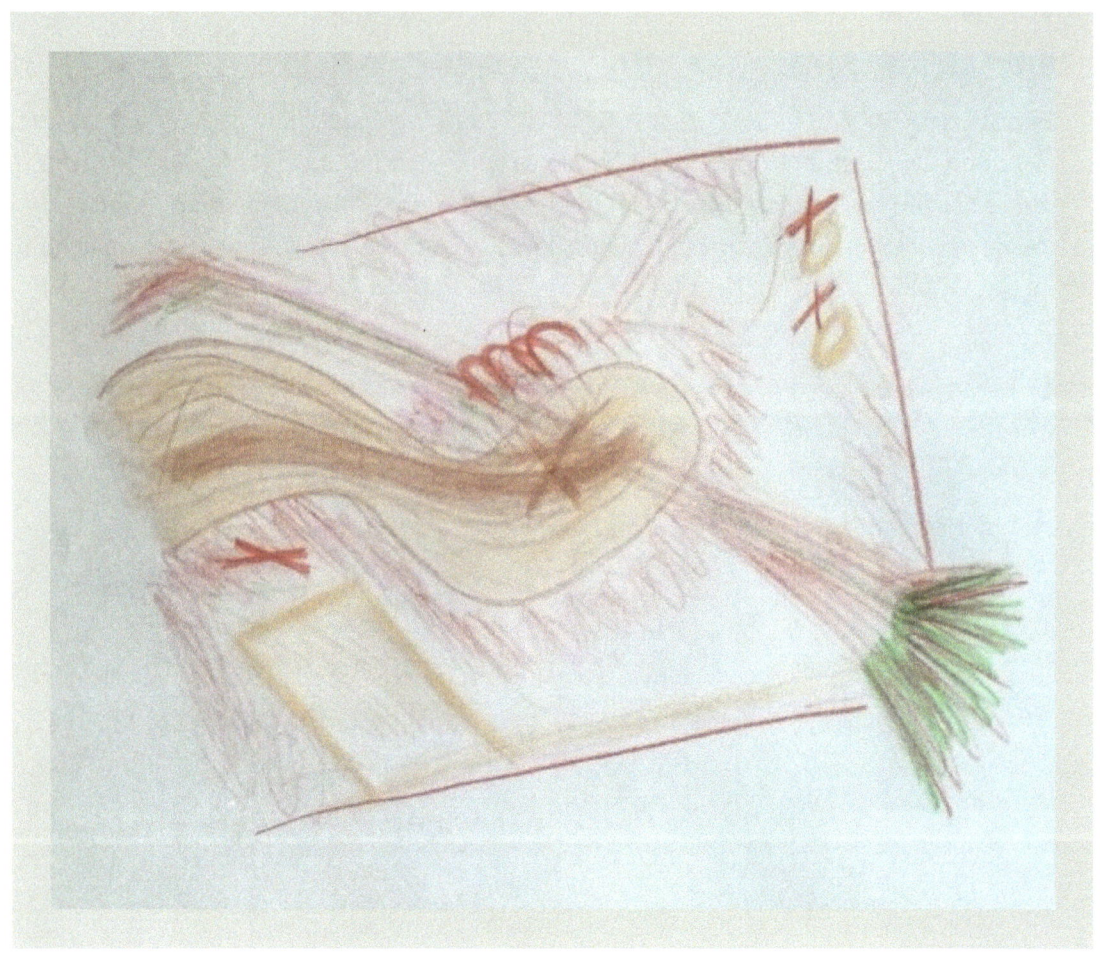

She isn't the only one with stories. She wants to hear yours. You can find her. You can tell her…

RosaLeeeLane@gmail.com
www.Amazon.com/author/readrllane

Oh. Listen. They said something last night about listening…

I can't remember what they said. They had said "both languages". I didn't know what they meant. I was flooded all night with their messages. It was an important day.

June 6, 2015

D-Day – In memoriam

June 6, 1944

The extra second

Of 2015

It is coming at the end of this month

"I would spend it with you, if I could." RL Lane

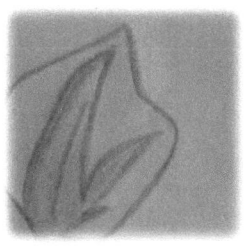

ISBN: 1514231255
ISBN-13: 978-1514231258

www.ingramcontent.com/pod-product-compliance
Lightning Source LLC
Chambersburg PA
CBHW050433180526
45159CB00006B/2517